BELLWETHER MEDIA • MINNEAPOLIS, MN

BLASTOFF! READERS 2

WORLD OF INSECTS

Stink Bugs

by Colleen Sexton

Note to Librarians, Teachers, and Parents:

Blastoff! Readers are carefully developed by literacy experts and combine standards-based content with developmentally appropriate text.

Level 1 provides the most support through repetition of high-frequency words, light text, predictable sentence patterns, and strong visual support.

Level 2 offers early readers a bit more challenge through varied simple sentences, increased text load, and less repetition of high-frequency words.

Level 3 advances early-fluent readers toward fluency through increased text and concept load, less reliance on visuals, longer sentences, and more literary language.

Level 4 builds reading stamina by providing more text per page, increased use of punctuation, greater variation in sentence patterns, and increasingly challenging vocabulary.

Level 5 encourages children to move from "learning to read" to "reading to learn" by providing even more text, varied writing styles, and less familiar topics.

Whichever book is right for your reader, Blastoff! Readers are the perfect books to build confidence and encourage a love of reading that will last a lifetime!

This edition first published in 2009 by Bellwether Media.

No part of this publication may be reproduced in whole or in part without written permission of the publisher. For information regarding permission, write to Bellwether Media Inc., Attention: Permissions Department, Post Office Box 19349, Minneapolis, MN 55419.

Library of Congress Cataloging-in-Publication Data
Sexton, Colleen A., 1967-
  Stink bugs / by Colleen Sexton.
    p. cm. – (Blastoff! readers) (World of insects)
  Includes bibliographical references.
  Summary: "Simple text and full color photographs introduce beginning readers to stink bugs. Developed by literacy experts for students in kindergarten through third grade"–Provided by publisher.
  ISBN-13: 978-1-60014-192-8 (hardcover : alk. paper)
  ISBN-10: 1-60014-192-7 (hardcover : alk. paper)
  1. Stinkbugs–Juvenile literature. I. Title.

QL523.P5S49 2008
595.7'54–dc22   2008019873

3 9082 11221 1225

Text copyright © 2009 by Bellwether Media Inc. BLASTOFF! READERS, TORQUE, and associated logos are trademarks and/or registered trademarks of Bellwether Media Inc.

SCHOLASTIC, CHILDREN'S PRESS, and associated logos are trademarks and/or registered trademarks of Scholastic Inc. Printed in the United States of America.

Contents

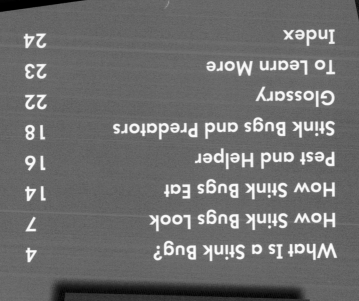

Stink bugs are **insects** that give off a strong smell when they are in trouble.

4

They live all over the world.
There are more than 5,000
different kinds of stink bugs.

Stink bugs lay eggs on leaves.

Young stink bugs hatch from eggs. They look very different from older stink bugs.

7

Most stink bugs match
the plants around them.
This helps them hide.

Other stink bugs have bright colors. These colors tell animals that they taste bad.

Stink bugs have four wings.

The wings fold around a bump on their backs.

Stink bugs have six legs.
Each leg has a claw to help
stink bugs hold on to plants.

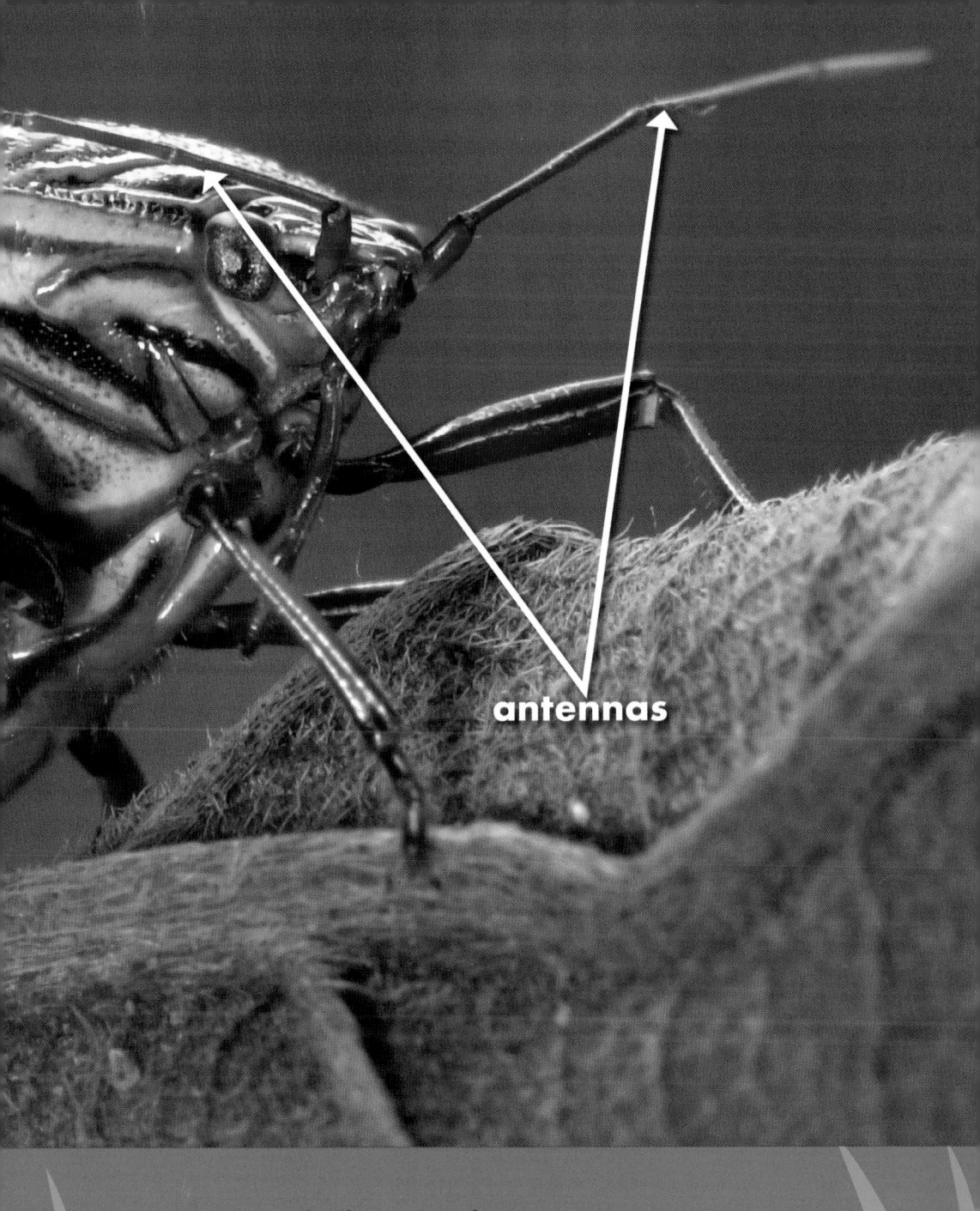

antennas

Stink bugs have two **antennas**. They use them to feel and smell.

mouth

Stink bugs have a mouth shaped like a tube. They can suck plant juices through it.

Some stink bugs eat other insects. They suck the guts out of them!

Stink bugs that eat plants can be **pests**. They destroy **crops**.

16

Stink bugs that eat insects
can save crops. They eat
other kinds of pests.

Birds, lizards, frogs, and
other animals hunt stink bugs.

Stink bugs try to scare away **predators**. They make loud sounds and wave their antennas.

19

Sometimes the predators won't go away. Then stink bugs give off a terrible smell.

Predators leave fast. They don't want to be around that bad smell. Would you?

Glossary

antennas—the feelers on an insect's head; insects use their antennas to touch and smell things.

crops—plants grown by people for food

insect—a small animal with six legs and a body divided into three parts; there are more insects in the world than any other kind of animal.

pests—insects that destroy or damage plants

predator—an animal that hunts other animals for food

To Learn More

AT THE LIBRARY

Kravetz, Jonathan. *Stink Bugs*. New York: PowerKids, 2006.

O'Neill, Amanda. *Insects and Bugs*. New York: Kingfisher, 2002.

Sydor, Colleen. *Raising a Little Stink*. Tonawanda, N.Y.: Kids Can Press, 2006.

ON THE WEB
Learning more about stink bugs is as easy as 1, 2, 3.

1. Go to www.factsurfer.com

2. Enter "stink bugs" into search box.

3. Click the "Surf" button and you will see a list of related web sites.

With factsurfer.com, finding more information is just a click away.

Index

The images in this book are reproduced through the courtesy of: photobar, front cover; JUNIORS BILDARCHIV / age fotostock, pp. 4-5, 10; Pete Oxford / Getty Images, p. 6; Kim Taylor / Getty Images, p. 7; Sommer, A / age fotostock, p. 8; Nick Garbutt / Getty Images, p. 9; Art Wolfe / Getty Images, p. 11; Piotr Naskrecki / Getty Images, pp. 12-13; Jose Antonio Jimenez / age fotostock, p. 14; Nigel Cattlin / Alamy, p 15; Criben, pp. 16-17; Frank B Yuwono, p. 18; Tim Gainey / Getty Images, p. 19; imagebroker / Alamy, pp. 20-21.